TRINITY
VOL.2 DEAD SPACE

TRINITY
VOL.2 DEAD SPACE

FRANCIS MANAPUL
CULLEN BUNN
writers

FRANCIS MANAPUL
SCOTT HANNA ＊ **SCOTT GODLEWSKI** ＊ **CLAY MANN** ＊ **EMANUELA LUPACCHINO**
MIGUEL MENDONÇA ＊ **JOHNNY DESJARDINS** ＊ **RAY McCARTHY**
artists

FRANCIS MANAPUL
WIL QUINTANA ＊ **BLOND** ＊ **BRAD ANDERSON** ＊ **HI-FI**
colorists

STEVE WANDS
TOM NAPOLITANO
letterers

FRANCIS MANAPUL
collection cover artist

SUPERMAN created by **JERRY SIEGEL** and **JOE SHUSTER**.
By special arrangement with the Jerry Siegel family.
BATMAN created by **BOB KANE** with **BILL FINGER**.
WONDER WOMAN created by **WILLIAM MOULTON MARSTON**.

EDDIE BERGANZA, PAUL KAMINSKI Editors - Original Series ∗ **JEB WOODARD** Group Editor - Collected Editions
ALEX GALER Editor - Collected Edition ∗ **STEVE COOK** Design Director - Books

BOB HARRAS Senior VP - Editor-in-Chief, DC Comics ∗ **PAT McCALLUM** Executive Editor, DC Comics

DIANE NELSON President ∗ **DAN DiDIO** Publisher ∗ **JIM LEE** Publisher ∗ **GEOFF JOHNS** President & Chief Creative Officer
AMIT DESAI Executive VP - Business & Marketing Strategy, Direct to Consumer & Global Franchise Management
SAM ADES Senior VP & General Manager, Digital Services ∗ **BOBBIE CHASE** VP & Executive Editor, Young Reader & Talent Development
MARK CHIARELLO Senior VP - Art, Design & Collected Editions ∗ **JOHN CUNNINGHAM** Senior VP - Sales & Trade Marketing
ANNE DePIES Senior VP - Business Strategy, Finance & Administration ∗ **DON FALLETTI** VP - Manufacturing Operations
LAWRENCE GANEM VP - Editorial Administration & Talent Relations ∗ **ALISON GILL** Senior VP - Manufacturing & Operations
HANK KANALZ Senior VP - Editorial Strategy & Administration ∗ **JAY KOGAN** VP - Legal Affairs ∗ **JACK MAHAN** VP - Business Affairs
NICK J. NAPOLITANO VP - Manufacturing Administration ∗ **EDDIE SCANNELL** VP - Consumer Marketing
COURTNEY SIMMONS Senior VP - Publicity & Communications ∗ **JIM (SKI) SOKOLOWSKI** VP - Comic Book Specialty Sales & Trade Marketing
NANCY SPEARS VP - Mass, Book, Digital Sales & Trade Marketing ∗ **MICHELE R. WELLS** VP - Content Strategy

TRINITY VOL. 2 DEAD SPACE

DC Comics, 2900 West Alameda Ave., Burbank, CA 91505
Printed by LSC Communications, Kendallville, IN, USA. 11/10/17. First Printing.
ISBN: 978-1-4012-7467-2

THE NEW PANDORAS

Cullen Bunn Script **Clay Mann** and **Miguel Mendonça** Pencils
Clay Mann and **Johnny Desjardins** Inks
Brad Anderson Colors **Steve Wands** Letters
Cover by **Mann** and **Steve Downer**
Paul Kaminski Associate Editor **Eddie Berganza** Group Editor

The Great Ruins.
60 Miles from the Kahndaqi Border.

Hhk!

Hrrrk!

SLLL

MORTALS.

ONE HAS ABANDONED THE VERY CONCEPT OF DEATH.

THE OTHER HAS DONE EVERYTHING IN HIS POWER TO *SEIZE* THE GIFTS OF THE GODS.

HELLO, BOYS.

I AM *CIRCE*.

YES-- *THAT* CIRCE.

BUT THEY ARE STILL MEN OF FLESH AND BLOOD.

FLAWED...

...AND, IN THIS CASE, *NECESSARY* FOR MY PLANS.

ARE THOSE--

--LAZARUS PITS?

NOT *QUITE*, PRECIOUS.

NOT QUITE.

...MALLEABLE TO MY WILL...

"PANDORA...CREATED BY THE GODS...

"BLESSED WITH MANY GIFTS BOTH *DIVINE* AND *CRUEL.*

"THE GODS GAVE HER A *BOX...* AND BADE HER NOT TO OPEN IT... BUT HER *CURIOSITY* WAS TOO GREAT.

"IN OPENING THE BOX, SHE UNLEASHED *EVIL* INTO THE WORLD.

"SICKNESS, FAMINE, PLAGUE...

"...AND OTHER, *MORE TERRIBLE THINGS.*

"SOME SAY PANDORA WAS STILL OUT THERE.

"SHE'S CHANGED...AS *TIMES* HAVE CHANGED.

"THE MALICIOUS FORCES SHE UNLEASHED HAVE CERTAINLY *ADAPTED* TO THE WORLD AROUND THEM.

SOME MIGHT EVEN SAY THAT *WE THREE* ARE PRODUCTS OF *PANDORA'S FOLLY.*

FOR NOW--YES!-- I NEED THEM.

FOR NOW.

EVEN AS I WORK WITH THE WITCH, I FEEL THAT I AM STUMBLING INTO SOME SNARE.

RA'S AL GHUL AND CIRCE.

AN ASSASSIN AND A SORCERESS.

I'LL NEVER SCRUB AWAY THE FILTH OF THIS ALLIANCE... ALBEIT A TEMPORARY ONE.

THAT'S IT!

THE PITS RECOGNIZE US!

THEIR BLESSINGS ARE OURS!

THE PANDORA PITS BELONG TO US!

"IT ALWAYS STARTS THE SAME WAY.

"A BEAUTIFUL DAY IN METROPOLIS.

"A NORMAL DAY.

"UNTIL IT ISN'T."

VWAAA-BOOOOM

WHAT WAS THAT?

E-EARTH-QUAKE?

CAME FROM--

LOOK! UP IN THE SKY!

IT'S A BIRD!

A PLANE!

N-NO! IT'S--

"OR NOT."

DIANA--

STAND DOWN--WHOEVER YOU ARE!

"YOU MIGHT HAVE BEEN MANIFESTATIONS OF *HOPE* AND *DOUBT*."

WONDER WOMAN!

LET ME GO!

HE'S COMING IN-- *FAST!*

LET GO OF THIS LIFE!

"WHAT IF WE WERE FIGHTING FOR A REALITY THAT WASN'T *OURS* IN THE FIRST PLACE?"

"IF *MY* WORLD...IF *HIS*...HAD BEEN TWISTED AND RESHAPED *ONCE*..."

UNF!

"...WHO WAS TO SAY IT HADN'T BEEN DONE A *HUNDRED TIMES?*"

"FOR ALL I KNEW, THERE WERE DOZENS OF FIGHTS--JUST LIKE THIS ONE--PLAYING OUT IN SOMEONE ELSE'S HEAD!"

PLEASE-- THE BOTH OF YOU--STAND DOWN!

LET'S AT LEAST FIGURE OUT WHY YOU'RE FIGHTING.

THEN YOU CAN GO BACK TO PUMMELING EACH OTHER!

"I'M UNSETTLED BY WHAT YOU'RE SAYING, CLARK."

I'M NOT SURE I LOVE THE IDEA THAT YOU HAVE VISIONS OF ME RUNNING AROUND INSIDE YOUR BRAIN.

THIS ISN'T THE TIME FOR *JOKES*, BRUCE.

WHO'S JOKING?

I KNOW HOW IT FEELS TO HAVE YOUR LIFE... YOUR HISTORY... EVERYTHING THAT MAKES YOU WHO YOU ARE...*TOYED* WITH.

WHAT IF IT WASN'T JUST ME?

WHAT IF *EVERYONE* HAS BEEN AFFECTED?

"...BECAUSE REALITY IS ON *THIN ICE*."

THIS CAN'T BE WHAT YOU WANT.

TAKE A BREATH, CLARK.

THINK FOR A SECOND.

LOOK AROUND. LOOK AT WHAT YOU'VE DONE.

"EVERYTHING WAS FALLING APART AROUND US.

"IT LOOKED LIKE METROPOLIS...

"...BUT I KNEW IT REPRESENTED SOMETHING MORE."

I BROUGHT YOU BOTH HERE BECAUSE I CAN'T STOP THINKING ABOUT WHAT HAPPENED.

Devil's Mouth Falls.
An hour north of Smallville.

THIS PLACE WAS SPECIAL TO YOU, CLARK. OF COURSE IT WILL BRING UP OLD MEMORIES.

I UNDERSTAND THIS MORE THAN ANYONE.

I KNOW WE WERE ALL TRAPPED IN MONGUL'S DREAM WORLD, BUT IT FELT SO REAL, DIANA.

REUNITING WITH MY FATHER, MEETING MY YOUNGER SELF, AND WE EVEN EXPERIENCED EACH OTHER'S CHILDHOODS. I FEEL LIKE THE THREE OF US GREW UP TOGETHER.

IT WASN'T, AND WE DIDN'T.

I KNOW, BUT THEN I THINK ABOUT THE CHILD BORN IN THAT DREAM, *THE WHITE MERCY.*

THAT PLACE WAS REAL TO HER, BRUCE.

THEN I THINK ABOUT HOW SHE SAVED US, AND WE COULDN'T SAVE HER.

SHE WASN'T REAL.

I KEEP TELLING MYSELF THAT, BRUCE...

...AND THEN I SAW THIS.

WHEN WE MET MY YOUNGER SELF IN THE DREAM WORLD, HE HID IN THIS CAVE.

HE CARVED OUT WHAT HE SAW THAT DAY.

IF THIS IS REAL...

THEN SHE COULD BE, TOO.

...AND WE LEFT HER IN THAT NIGHTMARE.

TARGETS ACQUIRED.

CYBORG'S BOOM TUBE?! BRUCE, DIANA, WE'D BETTER SUIT UP.

NOT A DREAM...

...THIS IS REAL.

I--I AM REAL.

SOMETHING OR SOMEONE HAS TAKEN OVER THE JUSTICE LEAGUE WATCHTOWER AND CUT OUT ITS POWER.

WE NEED TO FIND OUT WHO AND WHY.

BUT OUR NUMBER ONE PRIORITY IS GETTING VICTOR TO THE LOWER LEVELS OF THE SATALLITE.

DOWN THERE WE'LL FIND THE ESCAPE PODS. THEY OPERATE ON AN INDEPENDENT POWER SOURCE AND WE CAN USE IT TO JUMP-START VICTOR'S SYSTEMS.

WE'LL NEED TO CUT, BLAST AND TEAR THROUGH THIS ALIEN TECH THAT HAS TAKEN OVER THE HALLS OF JUSTICE.

IT'S A LONG SHOT THOSE PODS ARE STILL INTACT, BUT IT'S OUR ONLY HOPE OF SAVING VICTOR'S LIFE.

ONCE HIS SYSTEMS ARE BACK ONLINE, MAYBE HE'LL BE ABLE TO FILL US IN ON WHAT HAPPENED HERE.

IN THE MEANTIME, KEEP YOUR EYES PEELED. IT MAY BE MORE THAN JUST THE SHIP WHO TRIES TO KILL US.

I WAS TOO SLOW TO GRAB SUPERMAN AND WONDER WOMAN, BUT I FIGURED THEY CAN HOLD THEIR BREATH--

THEY'LL BE FINE. VICTOR'S ALIVE, BUT WE NEED TO GET HIM TO THE ESCAPE PODS IN THE LOWER LEVELS. FAST.

I'LL VIBRATE THE THREE OF US THROUGH THE FLOORS, BUT I'LL NEED A MINUTE TO RECOVER.

BARRY, WHAT THE HELL HAPPENED HERE?

THESE CREATURES LATCH ONTO A HOST AND TAKE OVER THE BODY. I'VE MANAGED TO STAY FREE OF IT BY KEEPING MY MOLECULES IN A CONSTANT STATE OF SEPARATION. I'VE BEEN VIBRATING FOR HOURS AND I'M JUST ABOUT READY TO PASS OUT.

SAY, YOU WOULDN'T HAPPEN TO HAVE A CANDY BAR IN ONE OF THOSE POUCHES OF YOURS?

THERE WAS A METEOR SHOWER THAT DAMAGED THE SHIP PRETTY BADLY.

VICTOR BOOMED US HERE TO HELP WITH SOME REPAIRS.

US?

WHO ELSE IS ON THIS SHIP?

"WELL, THERE WAS JESSICA. SHE WAS OUTSIDE FIXING A BREACH.

"WHEN SHE CAME BACK SOME KIND OF ALIEN CREATURE HAD LATCHED ONTO HER.

"I DON'T GET IT, THOUGH...GREEN LANTERNS SHOULD BE PROTECTED FROM THIS KIND OF THING.

"BEFORE WE KNEW IT, THE CREATURES WERE ALL OVER THE SHIP.

"IT GOT SIMON, TOO."

"IT TRIED TO LATCH ONTO CYBORG, BUT FOR SOME REASON IT DIDN'T TAKE.

"IT'S NOT OFTEN I SAY THIS, BRUCE, BUT I WAS GENUINELY AFRAID.

"YOU AND I...WE FIGHT CRIMINALS ON THE GROUND WITH ICE GUNS AND MAGIC WANDS.

"THESE ALIEN CREATURES DON'T TALK, THEY DON'T SEEM TO BE DRIVEN BY GREED OR OBSESSION OR ANY OTHER STUFF.

"THESE CREATURES JUST CONSUME AND ASSIMILATE..."

STORY, ART, COLORS AND COVER BY FRANCIS MANAPUL
LETTERS BY STEVE WANDS
ASSOCIATE EDITOR PAUL KAMINSKI EDITOR EDDIE BERGANZA

WITH EVERY PASSING SECOND OF INACTION, WE DESCEND CLOSER TO YOUR PLANET'S GRAVITATIONAL PULL. YOUR WATCHTOWER WILL CRASH AND RELEASE THE VIRUS, DESTROYING ALL LIFE-FORMS ON YOUR PLANET.

WE CAN SAVE THEM BY INITIATING MY VESSEL'S SELF-DESTRUCT FUNCTION. TO DO THAT, I NEED TO RESTORE ITS POWER BY SIPHONING YOURS. MY PROGRAMMING PREVENTS ME FROM LEAVING MY POST, WHICH IS WHY I NEED THE TWO OF YOU TO RESTART YOUR WATCHTOWER.

CYBORG... HE MUST HAVE SHUT DOWN THE POWER FOR THIS VERY REASON.

WE REJECT YOUR PROPOSAL, TRAVELER.

THERE IS ALWAYS ANOTHER WAY.

MAYBE WE CAN POWER UP THE WATCHTOWER AND STAY IN ORBIT WHILE WE FIGURE OUT WHAT TO--

NO! YOU ARE RUNNING OUT OF TIME.

HAVING NEVER EXPERIENCED CONFLICT, WE CREATED WEAPONS TO ERADICATE THE CREATURES AND THOSE INFECTED BY THEM.

BUT THEY ADAPTED AND GREW RESILIENT.

THOSE THAT SURVIVED WERE GATHERED IN THIS VESSEL, AND ONCE AT A SAFE DISTANCE FROM OUR PLANET, I WAS TO INITIATE ITS SELF-DESTRUCTION...

...BUT WE WERE CAUGHT IN A METEOR SHOWER AND SET ADRIFT FOR WEEKS.

WHICH BROUGHT US DIRECTLY TO YOU.

SCRREEEEEK

WHAT IS HAPPENING?!

OUR DESCENT HAS BEGUN. RESTART YOUR WATCHTOWER AND HELP ME COMPLETE MY MISSION.

IT IS TOO LATE FOR YOUR FRIENDS, BUT NOT FOR YOUR PLANET.

THE WATCHTOWER JUST GOT PULLED INTO EARTH'S ORBIT.

IT WON'T BE LONG BEFORE WE COME CRASHING DOWN!

SLAM

NO TELLING HOW LONG IT WILL BE BEFORE WE'RE INFECTED, TOO.

TIME IS RUNNING OUT.

AQUAMAN SAID TO "HELP THEM"? WHO'S HE TALKING ABOUT? THE ELECTRIC SHOCK SEEMED TO WORK FOR A BIT. MAYBE IF I--

DON'T EVEN THINK ABOUT VIBRATING THIS THING OFF HIM! WE DON'T KNOW HOW IT COULD AFFECT YOUR--

SMACK

OOMPH!

BEEP. BEEP.

CYBORG! HIS LIFE SIGNS ARE SLOWING DOWN! HIS SUIT WON'T SUSTAIN HIS HEART FOR MUCH LONGER!

YOU KNOW WE'RE AN UNLIKELY PAIR, BATMAN. YOU, ALL DARK AND BROODY, AND ME, BRIGHT AND UPBEAT.

WE'VE TAKEN DIFFERENT PATHS BUT ENDED UP ON THE SAME ROAD.

A ROAD LITTERED WITH OBSTACLES.

AND THE ONE THING THAT'S ALWAYS GOTTEN US THROUGH IS FAMILY.

GO BE WITH YOUR SON, BRUCE.

FLASH, DON'T--

FLASH! TAKE THIS BEFORE--

VRRRNN

HMMMPPH...

COME ON, CLARK, YOU CAN DO THIS. NUDGE THE JUSTICE LEAGUE WATCHTOWER JUST ENOUGH, THEN USE ITS OWN MOMENTUM TO SWING IT PAST EARTH.

THINK ABOUT JON...

...AND LOIS...

...AND THE BILLIONS OF LIVES DOWN BELOW--

HELP...

...US.

HELP THEM...

YOU ARE WASTING PRECIOUS TIME! YOUR COMRADE'S EFFORTS ARE MEANINGLESS!

SUPERMAN CAN SLOW THE TOWER'S MOMENTUM. THERE MAY STILL BE TIME TO--

NO!

WE MUST DESTROY BOTH OF OUR VESSELS, IT IS THE ONLY WAY TO STOP THEM ALL!

YOU DO NOT UNDERSTAND...

I *DO* UNDERSTAND.

ALL LIFE IS PRECIOUS.

WE *ALL* HAVE A PURPOSE.

EVEN THE MOST DANGEROUS CREATURES.

GREAT HERA!

THESE BEINGS... THEY ARE MORE THAN JUST A VIRUS, AREN'T THEY?

THEIR SHELLS ARE LIKE PUPAL SKINS... THEY WERE EVOLVING.

WHAT THEY ARE DOES NOT MATTER. THEY WERE DESTROYING OUR WAY OF LIFE!

HUNDREDS TURNED INTO THOUSANDS! THEY REPRODUCED SO QUICKLY, ALL WE COULD DO WAS CONTAIN THEM. WE USED THE LARGEST OF THEM TO DRAW THEM TO THIS VESSEL.

THEY WERE DRAWN TO A QUEEN... ACK!

THEIR MOTHER!

ARRrGHH!

YOU WANTED TO ALTER YOUR OWN WORLD'S NATURAL EVOLUTION.

AND YOU ENDED UP CREATING SOMETHING YOU COULD NOT CONTROL.

HOW DARE YOU! I...

FOR THE FIRST TIME EVER, YOUR PLANET FELT FEAR.

YOU HAVE BROKEN AN INTERGALACTIC TREATY THAT THE **GREEN LANTERN CORPS** WERE SURE TO ENFORCE. SO HERE YOU ARE, ATTEMPTING TO CLEAN UP ANY EVIDENCE OF YOUR PLANET'S INDISCRETION!

I WILL NOT ALLOW YOU TO USE OUR VERY OWN WATCHTOWER TO DESTROY ALL THESE LIVES.

BUT FIRST I MUST WARN MY FRIENDS AND PREVENT THIS STATION FROM CRASHING INTO *EARTH!*

THESE CREATURES HAVE GIVEN ME BACK MY MIND, AND I WILL HELP THEM REGAIN WHAT THEY'VE LOST.

GRAB

THESE PODS ARE POWERED INDEPENDENTLY FROM THE REST OF THE WATCHTOWER. IT SHOULD HAVE ENOUGH ENERGY TO REBOOT YOUR SYSTEM...

SKRRAAWWWK

...AND REGULATE YOUR HEART--

WORKING ALONE IS MY PREFERENCE, BUT I WOULDN'T COMPLAIN IF CLARK OR DIANA WERE HERE RIGHT NOW.

I HAVE TO ADMIT, GIANT MONSTERS INSIDE A FALLING SATELLITE ARE MORE THEIR FORTÉ.

BUT I SURE AS HELL CAN SAVE VICTOR...

SPLURCH

SPLURCH

...AND TRUST MY FRIENDS NOT TO LET US FALL.

IT'S NEVER EASY.

THE WORLD BELOW SEES ME AS INDESTRUCTIBLE.

POWERFUL BEYOND MEASURE.

THEY BELIEVE SUPERMAN WILL ALWAYS SAVE THE DAY.

BUT CLARK KENT KNOWS HE CAN'T ALWAYS DO IT ALONE.

THUMP

I BELIEVE IN THE POWER OF OTHERS...

VRRRRR

Mumbai, India.

"SUPERMAN, WONDER WOMAN, THIS CITY IS TOO DENSE! WE HAVE TO LAND THIS WATCHTOWER ON A ROOFTOP! CAN THE GREEN LANTERNS ASSIST?"

"THEY ARE BOTH PASSED OUT AT THE MOMENT. ON A POSITIVE NOTE, THE VIRUS THAT LATCHED ONTO THEM HAS *RELEASED* ITS GRIP!"

"YOU AND YOUR BRIGHT SIDE."

THE HEAT OF OUR RE-ENTRY INTO THE ATMOSPHERE HAS SPED UP THE VIRUS' METAMORPHOSIS!

WHAT... WHAT ARE THEY CHANGING INTO?

ANYTHING THAT DOESN'T HAVE TENTACLES...

IT WILL BE FINE. THE TRAVELER *LIED.*

THESE BEINGS, WHO CALL THEMSELVES *THE ENLIGHTENED,* THEY WERE ONLY DEFENDING THEMSELVES.

THERE, LEXCORP! ALL HIS BUILDINGS ARE EQUIPPED TO WITHSTAND...WELL, ME. IT SHOULD HOLD.

NGH!

NGH!

KRLUNNSE

WHAT ABOUT THE ENLIGHTENED AND THE TRAVELER?

THE TRAVELER WAS PROGRAMMED TO NEVER LEAVE HIS VESSEL. HE IS *DONE.*

KRFFFFFMM

EX

KRAAAAK

*Translated from Marathi. -- E&P

LE CORP

KRKK

⟨UP THERE!⟩

⟨WHOA!⟩

INITIATING...

TRINITY #10 Variant Cover by
BILL SIENKIEWICZ

TRINITY #11
Variant Cover by
BILL SIENKIEWICZ

A

RA'S in throne,
Circe at his
side, Lex on his
other

B

Ra's in front.
Lex stands on
rubble,skulls
AND the Trin-
ity in crumbles.
LEX hold out
superman as
he breaks
apart. Circe in
back doing a
spell

C

the three bad
guys up close
and the trinity
falling into
RA'S hand

COVER SKETCHES FOR
TRINITY #7 AND #8
BY Clay Mann

TRINITY #8 mann

A. gotham behind Batman,
Themyscira behind WW

B.

C.

COVER SKETCHES FOR TRINITY #9 AND #10
by Francis Manapul

#9

#10
A

#10
B